barcode →

Children of the World
Canada

For a free color catalog describing Gareth Stevens' list of high-quality children's books, call 1-800-341-3569 (USA) or 1-800-461-9120 (Canada).

For their help in the preparation of *Children of the World: Canada,* the writer and editors gratefully thank the Dennis family, Murray and Sandy Wright and their family, and John Saunders.

Picture credits: Covers, pp. 22-23, 32, 38 (upper), courtesy of the Dennis family; pp. 8-9, The Metro Toronto Convention & Visitors Association; pp. 18-19, © 1991, Gareth Stevens, Inc.; p. 33 (middle, bottom), Tourism New Brunswick, Canada; pp. 33 (upper), 48 (lower), Industry, Science and Technology Canada Photo; p. 48 (flag illustration), © Flag Research Center.

Library of Congress Cataloging-in-Publication Data

Wright, David K.
     Canada / by David K. Wright. — A Gareth Stevens Children's Books ed.
       p. cm. — (Children of the world)
     Includes bibliographical references and index.
     Summary: Looks at everyday life in modern-day Canada through the eyes of Rachel, a girl living in Halifax, Nova Scotia. Also surveys the civilization, history, culture, and geography of Canada.
     ISBN 0-8368-0256-X
     1. Canada—Juvenile literature. [1. Canada—Social life and customs. 2. Family life—Canada.] I. Title. II. Series: Children of the world (Milwaukee, Wis.)
     F1008.2.W75 1991
     971—dc20   89-43197

A Gareth Stevens Children's Books edition

Edited, designed, and produced by
Gareth Stevens Children's Books
1555 North RiverCenter Drive, Suite 201
Milwaukee, Wisconsin 53212, USA

Series editor: Valerie Weber
Research editor: Jennifer Thelen
Designer: Beth Karpfinger
Map design: Sheri Gibbs

Printed in the United States of America

1 2 3 4 5 6 7 8 9 97 96 95 94 93 92 91

Children of the World
Canada

Text and Photography
by David K. Wright

Gareth Stevens Children's Books
MILWAUKEE

. . . a note about *Children of the World*:

The children of the world live in fishing towns, Arctic regions, and urban centers, on islands and in mountain valleys, on sheep ranches and fruit farms. This series follows one child in each country through the pattern of his or her life. Candid photographs show the children with their families, at school, at play, and in their communities. The text describes the dreams of the children and, often through their own words, tells how they see themselves and their lives.

Each book also explores events that are unique to the country in which the child lives, including festivals, religious ceremonies, and national holidays. The *Children of the World* series does more than tell about foreign countries. It introduces the children of each country and shows readers what it is like to be a child in that country.

Children of the World includes the following published and soon-to-be-published titles:

Argentina	El Salvador	Japan	Singapore
Australia	England	Jordan	South Africa
Belize	Finland	Kenya	South Korea
Bhutan	France	Malaysia	Spain
Bolivia	Greece	Mexico	Sweden
Brazil	Guatemala	Nepal	Tanzania
Burma (Myanmar)	Honduras	New Zealand	Thailand
Canada	Hong Kong	Nicaragua	Turkey
China	Hungary	Nigeria	USSR
Costa Rica	India	Panama	Vietnam
Cuba	Indonesia	Peru	West Germany
Czechoslovakia	Ireland	Philippines	Yugoslavia
Egypt	Italy	Poland	Zambia

. . . and about *Canada*:

After living near a lake for most of her life, Rachel's back yard now ends on the ocean. Her family has moved from a town close to Toronto, in the middle of Canada, to the far eastern coast of this enormous country. Despite the move, Rachel's enthusiasm for rhythmic gymnastics remains. While she misses her friends and especially her gymnastics coach back near Toronto, Rachel adapts well to her new home, school, and friends, particularly her new Labrador puppy.

To enhance this book's value in libraries and classrooms, comprehensive reference sections include up-to-date information about Canada's geography, demographics, languages, currency, education, culture, industry, and natural resources. *Canada* also features a bibliography, a glossary, activities and research projects, and discussions of such subjects as Ottawa, the country's history, languages, political system, and ethnic and religious composition.

The living conditions and experiences of children in Canada vary according to economic, environmental, and ethnic circumstances. The reference sections help bring to life for young readers the diversity and richness of the culture and heritage of Canada. Of particular interest are discussions of the separatist movements and the diverse cultures of Canada.

CONTENTS

LIVING IN CANADA:
Rachel, a Girl on the Move

Rachel Dennis is 11 years old and beginning 6th grade. Her home is near Halifax, Nova Scotia, eastern Canada's largest city. Her back yard ends at the Atlantic Ocean! Rachel's family includes her father, Paul, who works in an office; her mother, Rhonda, who is a homemaker; and her brother, eight-year-old Greg, who is in the 4th grade.

Canadians are very mobile. So it's not surprising that Rachel's story really begins far away, near Toronto. . . .

Rachel Dennis enjoys a soft summer day near her former home north of Toronto. ▶

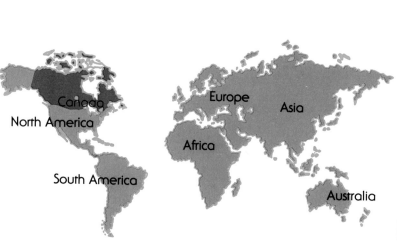

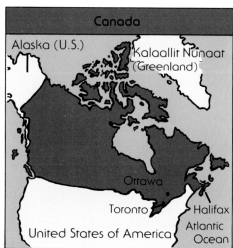

The CN Tower, the tallest freestanding structure in the world, dominates the Toronto skyline.

A Big Decision

Six months ago, no one in the Dennis family could have imagined being in Halifax. They lived more than 1,200 miles (1,900 km) west of this bustling seaport. Their large, new brick home was in a subdivision in Aurora, Ontario, just north of Toronto, Canada's biggest city. Toronto has more than 2.3 million residents and is the capital of Ontario, the most populous province in Canada. Paul worked for an electronics firm in Aurora.

The Dennis family poses on their front porch in Aurora, Ontario. Rachel's family includes her father, Paul; her mother, Rhonda; and her brother, eight-year-old Greg.

Rachel shares a photograph with her family. The kitchen is a popular gathering place for the Dennises.

One day, Rachel's grandfather — Paul's father — called from Halifax. He was planning to retire soon, and he wondered if Paul would like a job. The good news was, Paul could be his own boss in a business run by him and his younger brother, Peter. The bad news was, the Dennises would have to sell their home and move, leaving their friends behind.

Did they want to move? Their house in Aurora was just as everyone wanted it — bright, modern, comfortable, and convenient. Rhonda had spent hours and hours decorating. She ran a busy household and sometimes helped children and adults as a tutor. She was also very involved in Rachel's and Greg's school and after-school activities.

Paul had worked his way up in a company after starting there several years ago as a laborer. Before that, he had quit a job as a banker after he had been promoted to a position where he had to fire too many people.

Big plates of spaghetti provide the Dennises with lots of energy. That's Toni, a young visitor from Bulgaria, sitting next to Greg. She's in Canada to visit her aunt, who teaches Rachel rhythmic gymnastics.

Above: Spinning a ribbon, Rachel trains in a special gymnasium near her home. The gym has a soft rubber floor to prevent injuries.

Left: Greg waits for a pitch during a big game. Baseball is his favorite sport, and the Toronto Blue Jays are his favorite team.

Greg was on a winning softball team. He loved to play, hit the ball well, got on base often, and liked everything about the team but its colors! Both children had many neighborhood friends, but Rachel didn't see them often. She spent hours each week practicing rhythmic gymnastics.

13

What Is Rhythmic Gymnastics?

Rachel's many hours in the gym take some explaining. As a small child, she loved to play on jungle gyms. Other children and adults noticed her skill and energy. They told Rhonda that Rachel looked like a gymnast.

After a year of ballet classes, six-year-old Rachel joined a gymnastics class. For two years, she learned to do somersaults, back flips, and other difficult moves on the mats, bars, and beams. Suddenly, at age eight, it stopped being fun.

Rachel had realized that other children had injured themselves and she feared learning more. "I was scared," she admits. Her family saw rhythmic gymnastics while watching the 1988 Olympic Games on television. She has been working with balls, clubs, hoops, ribbons, and ropes ever since.

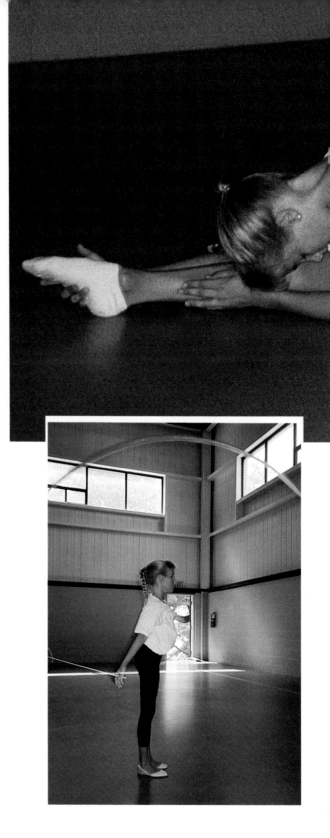

In meets, judges will grade Rachel on how she stands and moves, so she must concentrate.

14

Above: Can you do a split? Rachel can drop to the floor in this position almost instantly.

Right: Skipping rope is part of her routine.

Rhythmic gymnastics combines turns, jumps, and balancing with hand apparatus and is performed as music plays in the background. Pretty to watch, the sport is for girls only. The world's best rhythmic gymnasts today are from eastern Europe. One of them is Rachel's coach, Antoaneta Gabrovska.

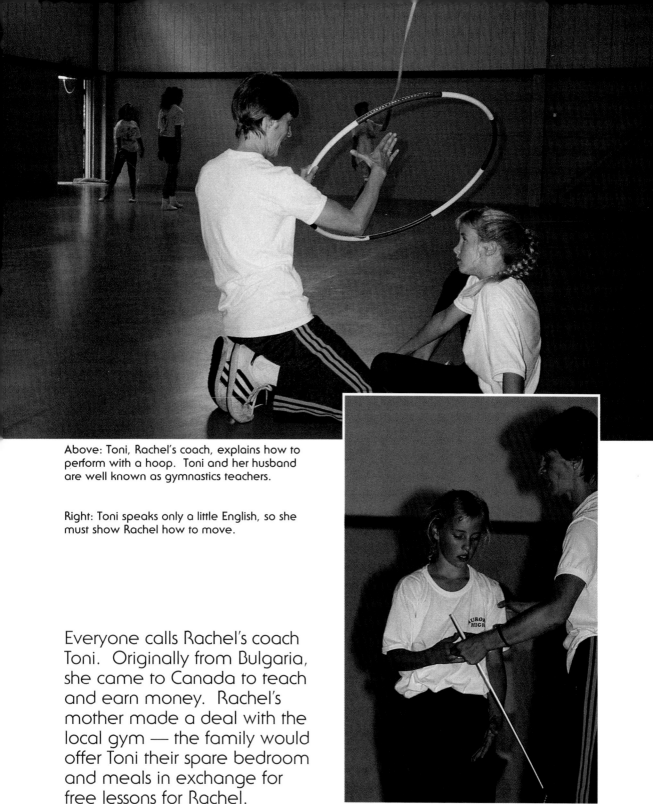

Above: Toni, Rachel's coach, explains how to perform with a hoop. Toni and her husband are well known as gymnastics teachers.

Right: Toni speaks only a little English, so she must show Rachel how to move.

Everyone calls Rachel's coach Toni. Originally from Bulgaria, she came to Canada to teach and earn money. Rachel's mother made a deal with the local gym — the family would offer Toni their spare bedroom and meals in exchange for free lessons for Rachel.

But Rachel learned more than rhythmic gymnastics from the older woman. At first, she thought Toni was nice at home and demanding inside the gym. But then Rachel found that Toni's sharp remarks and strong discipline during training would help her become a better performer. "I realized she really did like me, but she expected a lot," Rachel says.

Rachel trains 12 hours each week during school and 15 hours weekly in the summer. She's small and light for her age, ideal for gymnastics — but she has to watch her diet.

How much does Rachel weigh and how tall is she? Paul and Rhonda, who learned the English measurement system, say she weighs 70 pounds and stands four feet, seven and one-half inches. Rachel, who has learned the metric system, will say she weighs 31.8 kilograms and is 1.41 meters tall!

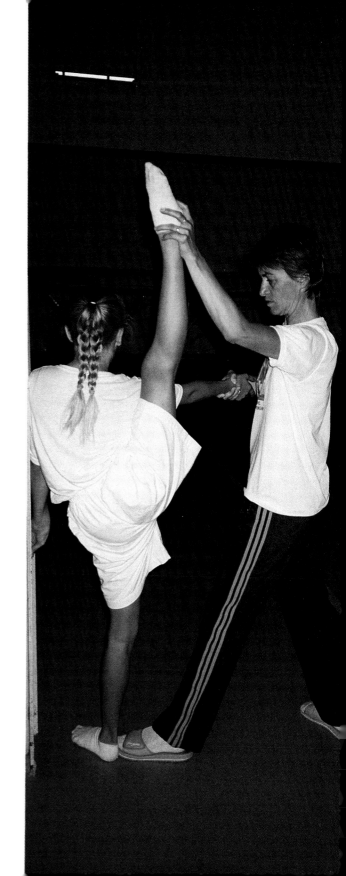

Rachel's left foot is at six o'clock and her right foot is at noon. The more flexible she is, the better she can perform.

The Diet of Champions

Rachel's favorite snack is sour-cream-and-onion potato chips. But she hardly ever eats such junk food. Instead, she enjoys big plates of spaghetti with meat sauce, or pizza, chicken, hot dogs, hamburgers, trout, or tuna. Her mother encourages her to eat all the bread, noodles, and vegetables she can hold. These foods give her energy without putting extra weight on her.

This morning, she eats toast covered with peanut butter and drinks apple juice. Rachel often makes her own breakfast, which may be waffles or pancakes or cereal. She has a good appetite and usually cleans her plate.

There are many clues in the Dennis kitchen that Canada is a bilingual country. Every can, jar, box, wrapper, and set of instructions made in Canada is printed in English and French.

A dreamy moment during a quick breakfast.

AROMA Nº1

JACOBS Café

Beau Jardin
Raspberry Preserves

NET WT. 13OZ. (368 G.)

new creamier
SKIPPY
CREAMY
Peanut Butter

COW BRAND.
baking soda
SODIUM BICARBONATE U.S.P.

bicarbonate de soude
BICARBONATE DE SODIUM U.S.P. · 500g

Fleur·de·Lait
NEUFCHATEL CHEESE
with
Herb & Spice

NOUVEAU
HYPOSODIQUE

NET 300g (10.6 oz)

LOW SALT

Petit
Beurre
FRENCH
BUTTER BISCUITS

NET WT.
28 OZ.

THE LITTLE SCHOOL
LE PETIT ECOLIER
Butter Biscuits Topped with
Pure Milk Chocolate
& Hazelnuts

An Expanding School

School is just four blocks away, and Rachel walks there with Greg and neighborhood friends. Aurora is one of the fastest-growing areas in all of Canada, so Regency Acres Public School combines a brick building with mobile classrooms, which are cheaper and quicker to erect than traditional school buildings. Rachel's room is in one of the mobile classrooms, which are also called portables or portable classrooms.

Regency Acres Public School is made up of this brick building and several portable classrooms.

Rachel likes school and does well. Her favorite subjects are music and language; she is an excellent writer. A ghost story she wrote and read to her class kept the boys and girls wide-eyed and silent. Right now, she says she would like to be a 4th- or 5th-grade teacher. Rachel also says she wants to be in the Olympic Games, but she must keep limber. Her mother says Rachel looks for ways to avoid her stretching exercises each morning.

School starts each year in early September and ends in late June. Holidays include Thanksgiving in October, two weeks off for Christmas and New Year's, four days off for Easter, and a week-long break in March. Regency Acres begins each weekday at 9 a.m. and ends at 3:30 p.m.

Rachel and Greg walk to school with two of their neighbors. ▶

Rachel's teacher, Shane Christensen, teaches his 28 5th-graders language arts, mathematics, history, music, art, social studies, science, French, and health and physical education. Because French is the first language of one out of every four Canadians, every public school student learns French. No one in Rachel's class speaks French at home, but some may know other languages. Six of Rachel's classmates were born in foreign countries, including Jamaica, Yugoslavia, and the Dominican Republic.

Canada has welcomed immigrants since its start because it is a huge country — the second largest on earth in area — with only about 27 million people. That means Canada has an average of only 6 people per square mile (2.3 per sq km). In comparison, China, the next largest country, has an average of 288 people per square mile (111 per sq km)!

My fifth grade class in

My best frog catch ever!

Rowing with Julie-Anne near my new home.

My new best friend, Julie-Anne.

What a meet, what a team!

ora.

Rachel's many photographs show her fun and friends in Aurora and Halifax.

Rachel makes up for a lack of wind by running.

Today, the children are flying kites they've made and decorated themselves. The designs feature everything from the Canadian flag with its huge red maple leaf to cartoon characters. Getting the kites up isn't easy — there's very little wind, and some of the kites are heavy. But Rachel and her classmates run back and forth, urging the kites skyward.

The maple leaf, Canada's symbol, is displayed proudly on this kite.

Rachel and her friends love the jungle gym.

The children eat lunch in 20 minutes in their classroom. Noise and laughter accompany the meal. Rachel says she likes "anything but peanut-butter-and-honey sandwiches." There is no cafeteria, so Rachel carries a sack lunch each school day. A sandwich, an apple, two cookies, and milk fill her up. Other children go home for lunch.

While many of the boys play baseball, Rachel and her friends play tag on the playground equipment. Several of the children move around the bars almost as quickly as Rachel. The game lasts 40 minutes, the entire noontime recess.

Several amusement parks are popular in the Toronto area. Rachel and Greg love the rides and are always eager to visit such parks.

Anxieties and Amusements

Rachel's parents have a plan to make the big move easier. They know how difficult it is for Rachel and Greg to pull up roots. So they reward the children for being good sports during all the changes by taking them to a huge park. Rachel and Greg love amusement parks and other big attractions, and their parents know that Halifax will have fewer of these than Toronto. Several of the children's friends meet them at the park, including Toni, the visiting niece of Rachel's gym coach. (Yes, they're both named Toni!)

Rachel and Toni climb aboard every thrilling ride where the line is short. They stop momentarily for a drink or a snack, then run to the next amusement.

Rachel's mother and father are being extra nice to the children prior to packing up, but they are also worried. They are afraid their home won't sell quickly and Paul will have to go to Halifax alone for a while. Just as it seems that their home in Aurora will never sell, the real-estate broker finds a buyer.

Left: Rachel, young Toni, Greg, and Rhonda wait in line to enjoy a ride.

Below: The Dennis house was sold just in the nick of time. Now, the family will be able to move before the start of school in the fall.

Last Days in Aurora

The family has lots to do before moving day. Paul and Rhonda must fly to Halifax and quickly choose their new home. Rachel and her dad will have to empty the water bed in her second-floor bedroom by letting the water run out her window. Packing gives Rachel and Rhonda a great chance to rummage through their closets and drawers.

Rachel also must learn a lot — and quickly — from Toni at the gym. Toni works her hard, refusing to smile when Rachel is funny or to offer a hand when the young gymnast collapses for a moment to regain her strength.

Rachel flops on the floor to regain her strength after hard training with the jump rope. She does routines over and over to improve her performance.

But it isn't all work. Rachel chats with Toni and learns that she has found an apartment. Soon, her husband will join her and they will both teach gymnastics in Aurora. Rachel devours a quick carryout lunch of a pita sandwich and a bottle of soda, then jumps just for fun on the trampoline.

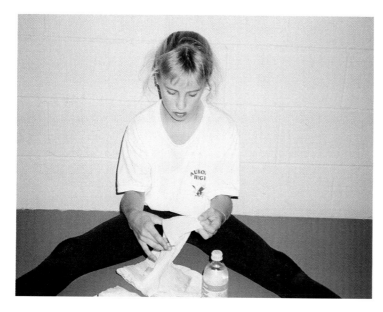

Above: With the breeze from an open door to cool them, Rachel and Toni work with the long ribbons.

Left: Lunch at the gym is a fast sandwich and a soft drink.

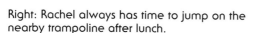

Right: Rachel always has time to jump on the nearby trampoline after lunch.

Rachel loves the miniature horses that graze in her friend Robbie's corral.

After practice one day, Rachel goes home with Robbie, who takes lessons in another part of the gym. Robbie's home is on a farm with lots of animals, including miniature horses and a fluffy cat. But the two friends are just as fascinated by a passing frog!

Rachel and Robbie go for a ride around the yard on his all-terrain vehicle, hop on his trampoline, and take a swim. Despite all of the animals and fancy equipment, the two most enjoy running through the tall corn that grows behind Robbie's house. Their scampering ends when the two think they see a wolf! They run as fast as they can back to the house. Robbie's mother says that a pack of wolves roams the area in winter.

The two friends cruise the yard on Robbie's all-terrain vehicle.

Robbie has his own trampoline and Rachel can't stay away from it.

Robbie is a year younger than Rachel. The two became friends because they both like gymnastics and often met at the gym. They will miss each other when Rachel moves.

The day is warm, so the two friends take a dip in Robbie's pool.

A Move, a New Home

Rachel will also miss Toni. They say good-bye, but they may see each other during school vacations. Rachel wants to return to Toronto during vacations to train with the Bulgarian coach. But her mother knows that Rachel hasn't seen Halifax, so she doesn't realize that she will have a life there, too.

The Dennis family watches the movers pack their belongings. Then, they hop in the car for 22 hours of driving. The three-day drive takes them through Quebec, where most signs are in French, and past Montreal, North America's largest French-speaking city.

Fortunately, movers will do most of the heavy lifting.

The St. Lawrence flows eastward toward the Atlantic. Rachel can practice her French with the billboards not far from the river.

For part of the trip, their route, the Trans-Canada Highway, runs along the St. Lawrence River. Once the road turns away from the river, the land becomes hilly. Lakes, pine trees, and miles of scenic open countryside with few homes or farms contrast with the more populated Ontario. The family loves to camp out, so the trip is almost a vacation.

The area where Rachel now lives is beside a series of small saltwater bays and inlets.

Halifax and Nova Scotia

The province of Nova Scotia is on a peninsula that sticks out into the Atlantic Ocean. About 115,000 people live in Halifax, the capital, and about 65,000 live in Dartmouth, the city that faces Halifax across a deep harbor.

The harbor is important both in Canada's history and to its economy. Ships from Europe and throughout the world unload goods in Halifax. In addition, during World Wars I and II, huge fleets of warships gathered in Halifax for the dangerous trip across the Atlantic. During World War I, an ammunition ship collided with another ship in the harbor. The resulting explosion killed more than 1,650 people.

That's Halifax in the distance. The view is from Dartmouth, on the opposite side of the harbor.

This pretty scene shows the Dennis family boathouse and back yard on a scenic September morning. It's very different from Ontario!

Fortunately, things are much quieter nowadays. The Dennises' new home is on a cove just in from the coast, about 15 miles (24 km) west of Halifax Harbor. Besides a beautiful view, their new home has a boat and a boathouse. It also has a new member of the family.

Rachel and Huggy Bear are instantly in love!

Hello, Huggy Bear

Huggy Bear flew all the way from western Canada to become part of the Dennis family. She is a Labrador puppy, a gift from Rachel and Greg's aunt and uncle. Labradors love to swim, and Huggy Bear proves it by eagerly fetching sticks thrown into the salty water. She plays with the children until she runs out of breath.

Rachel doesn't have to teach Huggy Bear to fetch — the dog will run after anything anyone throws.

Everyone loves the dog. Paul even forgives her for gnawing on his slippers, and Rhonda has big plans for her. As a girl, Rhonda owned and showed horses. She loves to be around animals and enjoys training them. Labs are smart, so training should be easy. Like Rachel, Huggy Bear may soon be performing!

Once his slippers are safe from sharp puppy teeth, Paul takes the children out in the boat. It isn't new and requires some repairs, but it is fun to drive. The only problem is, it's six inches (15 cm) too long to fit in the boathouse! Where will the boat be stored in the winter? It can't be left in the water, even though salt water does not freeze as easily as fresh water. This is a problem that Paul can ignore for a while.

Greg and Rachel must have life jackets on before Paul will take the family boat for a cruise.

A Family Gathering

Rachel's dad now works in offices above a shopping center in a Halifax neighborhood. He is learning from his father how to sell big pieces of machinery to electric companies.

One of the nice things about living in Halifax is being near Paul's parents. Paul and his brother Peter often go home with their father for one of their mother's delicious lunches. Today, she serves them a huge macaroni-and-cheese casserole, tossed salad, and peach pie. Rachel's grandmother was born in New-foundland, a rough and rugged province to the north. Her children tease her about being a "Newfie," which is what other Canadians affectionately call a person from Newfoundland.

Rachel's dad and her grandfather are now in the same business, although Grandfather is easing gradually into retirement.

Rachel's father's side of the family includes Grandfather Dennis, standing, and Grandmother Dennis, seated on the right. From left are Uncle Michael and his wife, Aunt Sharon; Uncle Peter, Paul's younger brother; and Paul. These reunions of the brothers are rare, since Michael and Sharon live thousands of miles west, in Alberta.

This is a fun occasion since Paul's oldest brother, Michael, and his wife, Sharon, are visiting, too. They brought Huggy Bear from their home in Edmonton, Alberta, where they raise and board dogs. Everyone is glad to see everyone else and looks forward to getting together at Rachel's new house this evening.

Everyone here shares the same last name — Dennis. Rachel and her relatives join Huggy Bear on the porch before grilling hamburgers and hot dogs at Rachel's new home.

◀ Rachel attacks her homework as soon as she gets off the bus. Today, she's learning about the Micmac Native Canadians, the original residents of Nova Scotia.

That afternoon, Rhonda greets the children as they run in the door. Rachel immediately starts her homework. She has about an hour of work each afternoon or evening. "I thought by the 6th grade it would be hard, but it's still fun," she says.

Her class is studying the Micmac Native Canadians. This tribe was living in Nova Scotia when the first Europeans arrived. Rachel has to decide if she would like to live as the Micmacs did, then write her answer. She scours magazines for photos of animals that were used in different ways by the Micmacs. She pastes animal pictures between her paragraphs.

Meanwhile, Rhonda counts hamburger patties, hot dogs, buns, and side dishes for the visitors. They arrive at about the same time as Paul, who shows them around and introduces his parents and Peter to Huggy Bear.

Boutiliers Point School

Rachel and Greg are groggy the next morning, but breakfast seems to awaken them. After a quick meal of waffles, they comb their hair, brush their teeth, and get their schoolwork together. They must walk a block away to wait for the school bus. The bus stop is across the street from the home of Patrick, a new friend, so the three swing on the rope in Patrick's front yard until they hear the bus turn a corner.

Rachel and Greg have fun waiting for the morning bus by swinging in a neighbor's yard.

They hear the bus turn a corner and run to the bus stop just in time. Their ride lasts about 15 minutes.

Rachel and Greg attend Boutiliers Point School. This public school holds 70 4th-, 5th-, and 6th-grade students. Rachel has made friends fast, but Greg is small and a bit shy. "Some of these kids play tackle basketball," he says, rolling his eyes. He's also concerned that the boys will like soccer better than baseball.

Rachel's teacher is Lori McIsaac. She has 20 6th-graders, 12 boys and 8 girls. Mrs. McIsaac teaches social studies, science, writing, reading, and mathematics. The children visit other teachers for art, French, band, and health and physical education.

Rachel's 6th-grade class at Boutiliers Point School.

Social studies class is fun, as several students discuss whether they would like to live like the Micmacs. Indian life fascinates them. Many of the children love the outdoors and enjoy camping out. They also love to dance. But Rachel decides that "I could never eat raw moose."

During the period set aside for reading, Rachel avidly reads *Charlotte's Web*. Mrs. McIsaac always stacks plenty of books on the library table in the back of the room. The children check out the books and read to themselves.

Keeping the children interested in reading is one of Mrs. McIsaac's goals.

Silent reading takes up at least 20 minutes of every school day.

Recess reveals that Rachel has already made many friends. They sit on a guardrail and talk and laugh.

At recess, Rachel and three of her friends run up the hill above the school and nibble a snack while they sit on a metal railing. They look down on children playing kick-ball and other games in the school yard. The day is warm and sunny, and from the hill, Rachel can see the cove near her home. At this moment, she may have forgotten Toronto, Aurora, and her long hours of training in the gym.

FOR YOUR INFORMATION: Canada

Official Name: Canada

Capital: Ottawa

History

Across a Land Bridge

The first humans to arrive in Canada came from Asia. Wrapped in animal skins, they walked across a frigid bridge of land between Asia and North America. Hunter-gatherers, they arrived in North America between 25,000 and 10,000 BC. These Indians were followed from Asia by a second group of immigrants that later were known as the Inuit (Eskimos). The Inuit were used to the arctic cold and stayed far to the north while Indian tribes spread south and east from Alaska, across Canada and the United States, into Mexico and throughout South America. Melting glaciers caused the land bridge to disappear beneath rising Bering Sea water after 10,000 BC.

The third longest river in Canada, the St. Lawrence flows through the peaceful countryside of Quebec.

Indians lived in forests and on plains from the Arctic ice south. They survived on salmon, deer, rabbit, game birds, buffalo, beaver, caribou, and waterfowl. They also gathered corn, apples, squash, and nuts or, in the south where the soil was rich, had permanent farms and houses. Huge distances separated individual tribes, causing vast differences in languages and cultures.

Nordic sailors from Greenland and Iceland showed up about AD 1000. They beached their boats on the rocky Atlantic coasts of Newfoundland and Nova Scotia. Fishing villages sprang up, only to be abandoned a few years later. Epic poems named the coast Vinland, meaning "Wineland," because of the wild grapes found growing there, and told of its discovery by adventurers such as Leif Ericson.

In 1497, five years after the voyage of Columbus, an Italian named John Cabot claimed Newfoundland for England. Cabot had been hired to look for the Northwest Passage — a way to sail west from Europe to Asia. Instead, he told of a cold and damp land surrounded by seas so filled with fish they nearly stopped his boat. French, English, Spanish, and Portuguese fishermen soon brought fishing fleets over and built fishing huts on the Atlantic coast.

The French Explore Canada

In 1534, Jacques Cartier, a French explorer, sailed up the St. Lawrence River as far as today's city of Quebec. Cartier found Indians eager to trade valuable furs for cheap trinkets, knives, and hatchets. Cartier named Canada "New France" and returned with settlers in 1541. But disease, poor leadership, and bitter weather caused his colony on the St. Lawrence to fail.

For several decades, Canada's native people again had the country to themselves. Then, in 1604, Samuel de Champlain started the French village of Port Royal on the Nova Scotia coast. The French named the area Acadia. Champlain then pushed westward. He began a settlement where Quebec now stands and explored as far as modern-day Ontario. He also shot several Iroquois tribe members to aid the Algonquin Indians in their war against the Iroquois, setting the scene for future confrontations. Champlain returned to France with wonderful furs and detailed maps, impressing Europe with tales of riches and the great size of the New World.

Furs soon brought to Canada the *coureurs de bois*, or forest runners. These tough French woodsmen often traveled with missionary priests who taught the Roman Catholic religion to the Indians, undermining the old systems of belief. Pushing up thundering rivers or hiking through the bush, the adventurers came to be known as *voyageurs* for their canoe voyages or trips.

They had to overcome brutal winters and the now-hostile Indians to collect furs and help the trading companies grow rich.

Britain Stakes Its Claim

The British soon became interested in Canada. They watched in 1610 as Henry Hudson explored the huge interior bay later named after him. In 1621, the first British settlement began on Nova Scotia. British settlers soon tried to push the French west. Britons also muscled in on the fur trade by starting the Hudson's Bay Company in 1670.

Wars without winners took place in Europe at this time and echoed in North America. The British and the French shoved each other around, capturing and recapturing towns and lands. One result was that the French handed the British their colony of Acadia in 1713. French-speaking Acadians were forced to leave their homes and farms.

By 1744, France had claimed territory as far west as the Saskatchewan River. A string of French forts held midwestern Canada and today's central United States. French defenders were joined by powerful and warlike Indians while the British were aided by American colonists. Despite many fierce battles, by 1763, France had formally surrendered all territory in Canada.

Thousands of American colonists loyal to Britain fled the fledgling United States for Canada during the Revolutionary War in the 1770s. Revolutionary troops also invaded at this time, but Britain stayed in control. In 1791, Britain divided the old French colony into French-speaking Lower Canada and English-speaking Upper Canada to allow the use of both English and French law. It gave both areas some representative government, allowing citizens who owned property to elect an assembly.

After an invasion by the United States during the War of 1812 failed, settlers in Canada spent most of the 19th century trying to tame their huge country — and rebelling successfully for more freedom from Great Britain. English, Scottish, and Irish immigrants came by the thousands. As Canada became a united British colony in 1841, farmers began to plow the huge western prairie and plant wheat. More immigrants arrived from Germany, the United States, eastern Europe, and Russia.

The British North America Act

The year 1867 is important in Canadian history. That year, the British North America Act gave several of the provinces self-government when they joined to become the Dominion of Canada. Sir John A. Macdonald, who designed much of the new government, was named the first prime minister.

Lumbering and fishing industries sprang up from coast to coast, encouraging the opening up of land previously uninhabited by Europeans. More homesteaders arrived.

But not everyone was happy. French-Indian trappers and frontiersmen saw farmers ruining their land and rebelled against the taming of their wilderness. Indians who had been pushed onto reservations also rebelled. Their last uprising ended in 1885 when French-Indian leader Louis Riel was hanged and Indian leaders Big Bear and Poundmaker were captured. That same year, the Canadian Pacific Railroad was completed from the Atlantic to the Pacific, opening up new territory for farming and industries.

The Wars: Rich to Poor and Back Again

The big news as the 20th century drew near was gold. The Klondike Gold Rush of 1896 lured thousands of prospectors to Canada's frigid Yukon Territory. Other mining ventures, rich prairie land, and heavy industry soon made Canada a wealthy country.

Canada contributed greatly to Allied victories in World War I and World War II. Troops and munitions poured out of Canada into the Pacific and European war effort. While the Canadian army often acted as shock troops on the ground, the Royal Canadian Air Force became famous for its daring and accurate fighter pilots. The Canadian navy sank many enemy ships while protecting war supply ships.

Between the wars, though, the worldwide Great Depression hit Canada hard. The problems of unemployment and low wages were worsened by a drought in the western provinces, where people fled farms that had turned to dust. By 1935, 20% of the population depended on government relief. By providing the need for new industries such as shipbuilding and munitions, World War II saved the Canadian economy.

Defending the Continent

After World War II, Canada cooperated with the United States in putting radar stations all across the far north. This was the era of the cold war, and these stations were to warn North America if Soviet planes or missiles were coming. Today, Canada is a member of the United Nations and the North Atlantic Treaty Organization (NATO).

Canada is known for its good government, made up of calm, educated, and reasonable people. One was William Lyon Mackenzie King, who ran the Liberal political party from 1921 until his death in 1950. He also served as Canada's prime minister three times, for a total of 22 years. He moved the country ahead by getting many different kinds of Canadians to agree on important issues and by keeping the country united during the war years.

The country as it appears on modern maps did not take shape until 1949. That was the year Newfoundland became a province, boosting the number of provinces to ten and the number of territories to two.

Independence for Quebec?

Although interrupted by World War II, the flood of immigration continued. The country earned a worldwide reputation for giving shelter to Jews, Chinese, Vietnamese, Pakistanis — groups uprooted from their homelands.

Some Québecois (persons living in Quebec) resented the newcomers as the percentage of French-speaking Canadians grew smaller. Pockets of French culture shrank as each province grew in population. In 1968, the newly formed Parti Québecois announced its aim to make Quebec an independent republic. But in 1980, Quebec voters chose to remain part of Canada.

Yet ill feeling between Québecois and other Canadians remains. In 1990, the country's nine other provinces failed to give Quebec special privileges to preserve and promote Quebec as a distinct society. Many of its French-speaking citizens threatened once again to seek independence. If this happens, it will set a precedent for other provinces and ethnic groups to split off from the confederation.

Government

Canada's form of government is a confederation with parliamentary democracy. Confederation means that the country's ten provinces and two territories form a single, national government. Parliamentary democracy means that the people of Canada elect the representatives to the parliament that governs them. Canada's Parliament has two legislative houses, the Senate and the House of Commons. The Senate has 112 members and the more powerful House has 295.

Elections are held at least every five years, with citizens 18 or older eligible to vote. Elections can be held sooner if citizens seem to be losing confidence in their government.

As in Great Britain, there is a formal head of state and a prime minister. Both seek advice from a small group of experts chosen by the prime minister and known as the cabinet. The governor general is the formal head of state and traditionally has been the representative of Britain's monarch. The prime minister is elected, has the real political power, and runs the country.

Canada's court system also plays a major role in government. It interprets the law in disputes between individuals and between different agencies of government. The highest court is the Supreme Court of Canada, made up of nine justices, all appointed by the governor general on the advice of the cabinet. By law, three of the nine must come from the Province of Quebec.

Historically, provincial governments in Canada have had large shares of power. This was because Canada was so huge that a federal government could not extend across most of North America. To better define the federal government's job, the Constitution Act was passed in 1982. It allowed Canada to amend its constitution without Britain's approval and allowed provinces to not comply with amendments with which they did not agree.

There are several major political parties in Canada. The Progressive Conservatives are usually, but not always, English-speaking, and tend to feel that farmers' interests are being neglected in favor of those of large corporations. Liberals, who believe that the provinces should have more power, are strong in the east, including Quebec. The New Democratic party, which believes in government ownership of public utilities and transportation, has a large following in the prairie provinces.

Citizens complain most about prices and taxes, which are extremely high. For example, a recent survey showed that it cost more to live in Toronto than in any other city in North America!

Natural Resources

Canada is wealthy in many ways. Large mineral deposits of gold, silver, uranium, platinum, copper, nickel, zinc, lead, and iron ore and big reserves of oil and natural gas lie beneath its soil. Much of this underground wealth is only now being discovered because it is in the remote Northwest Territories.

Spruce, balsam, pine, and other hardy trees cover about 48% of the country's land. Along the western coast are also big stands of cedar, hemlock, and fir. Lumber, paper, and other wood products account for about 15% of all exports, and many of these products are sent to the United States. Fishing is also a major industry on both coasts.

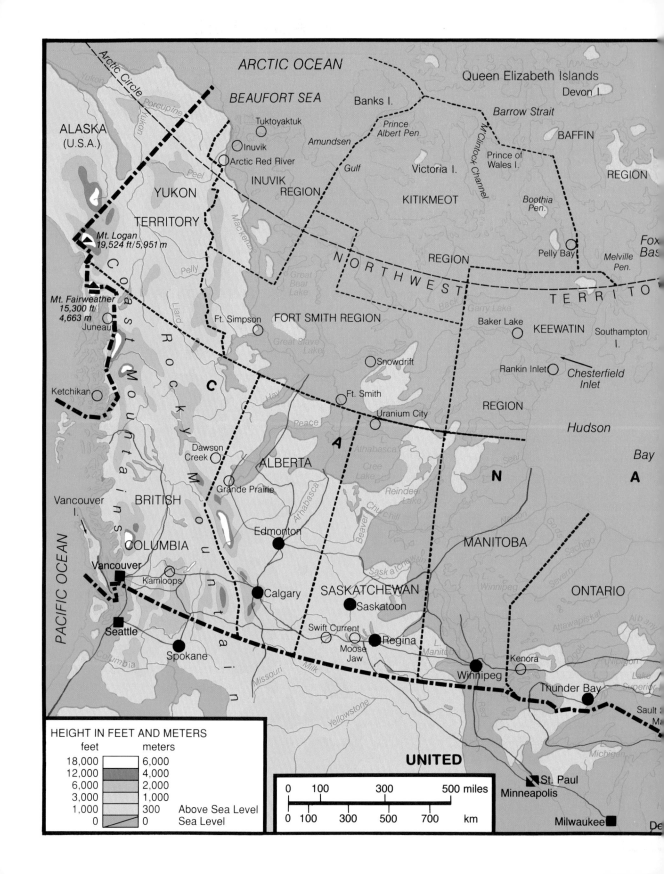

ARCTIC OCEAN

BEAUFORT SEA

Queen Elizabeth Islands

Devon I.

Banks I.

Barrow Strait

ALASKA
(U.S.A.)

Tuktoyaktuk

*Prince
Albert Pen.*

BAFFIN

M'Clintock Channel

Inuvik

Amundsen

Prince of
Wales I.

REGION

Arctic Red River

Gulf

Victoria I.

YUKON

INUVIK

*Boothia
Pen.*

REGION

KITIKMEOT

TERRITORY

N O R T H W E S T

Mt. Logan
19,524 ft/5,951 m

Pelly Bay

*Melville
Pen.*

Fox
Bas

REGION

Mt. Fairweather
15,300 ft/
4,663 m

*Great
Bear
Lake*

T E R R I T O

Juneau

Ft. Simpson

FORT SMITH REGION

Garry Lake

Baker Lake

KEEWATIN

*Southampton
I.*

*Great Slave
Lake*

Snowdrift

Rankin Inlet

*Chesterfield
Inlet*

Ketchikan

C

Ft. Smith

REGION

Hudson

Uranium City

Peace

Bay

Dawson
Creek

ALBERTA

A

Athabasca

*Cree
Lake*

N

A

Grande Prairie

BRITISH

*Reindeer
Lake*

Vancouver
I.

Churchill

Edmonton

MANITOBA

ONTARIO

COLUMBIA

PACIFIC OCEAN

Vancouver

Kamloops

Calgary

SASKATCHEWAN

Saskatoon

Seattle

Swift Current

Regina

Kenora

Spokane

Moose
Jaw

Winnipeg

Thunder Bay

Sault

HEIGHT IN FEET AND METERS

feet   meters
18,000   6,000
12,000   4,000
6,000   2,000
3,000   1,000
1,000   300   Above Sea Level
0   0   Sea Level

UNITED

0   100   300   500 miles

0 100 300 500 700 km

St. Paul
Minneapolis

Milwaukee

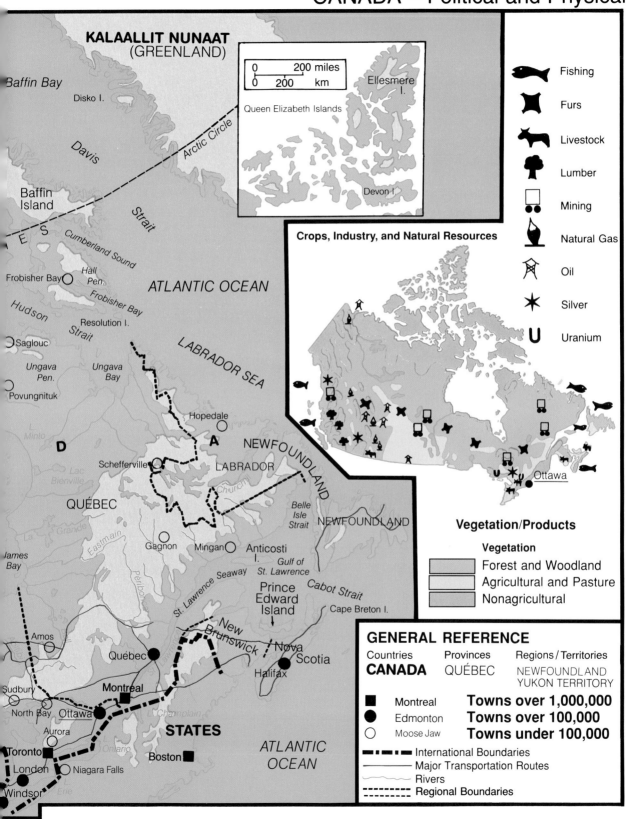

CANADA – Political and Physical

KALAALLIT NUNAAT (GREENLAND)

Baffin Bay

Disko I.

Davis

Baffin Island

Arctic Circle

Cumberland Sound

Strait

Frobisher Bay ○

Hall Pen.

Frobisher Bay

ATLANTIC OCEAN

Hudson

Saglouc ○

Resolution I.

Strait

Ungava Pen.

Ungava Bay

Povungnituk ○

LABRADOR SEA

Hopedale ○

L. Minto

D

A

NEWFOUNDLAND

Lac Bienville

Schefferville ○

LABRADOR

QUÉBEC

La Grande

Eastmain

Gagnon ○

Mingan ○

Church

Anticosti I.

Belle Isle Strait

NEWFOUNDLAND

James Bay

Peribol

St. Lawrence Seaway

Gulf of St. Lawrence

Prince Edward Island

Cabot Strait

Cape Breton I.

Amos ○

New Brunswick

Québec ●

Nova Scotia

Sudbury ○

Montréal ■

Halifax ●

North Bay ○

Ottawa ○

Aurora ○

STATES

ATLANTIC OCEAN

Toronto ■

Ontario

Boston ■

London ○

Niagara Falls ○

Windsor ●

L. Erie

Inset map
0 — 200 miles
0 — 200 km

Queen Elizabeth Islands

Ellesmere I.

Devon I.

Crops, Industry, and Natural Resources

Ottawa

Legend
Fishing	
Furs	
Livestock	
Lumber	
Mining	
Natural Gas	
Oil	
Silver	
U	Uranium

Vegetation/Products

Vegetation

Forest and Woodland
Agricultural and Pasture
Nonagricultural

GENERAL REFERENCE

Countries	Provinces	Regions / Territories
CANADA	QUÉBEC	NEWFOUNDLAND YUKON TERRITORY

■ Montreal — **Towns over 1,000,000**
● Edmonton — **Towns over 100,000**
○ Moose Jaw — **Towns under 100,000**

▪–▪–▪ International Boundaries
—— Major Transportation Routes
～～ Rivers
▪▪▪▪ Regional Boundaries

Language

Canada is a bilingual country. Every consumer product made in the country is labeled in English and French. English and French are taught to all elementary schoolchildren, except in Quebec, where most schools are French.

The country named English and French the official languages in 1969. This was done in part to keep Canada together and to treat French-speaking Canadians equally. Changing the words on every federal building and all federal notices since then has cost more than $4.5 billion! There are many parts of Canada today where no one speaks French and places, mostly in Quebec and New Brunswick, where no one speaks English. Recently, Quebec passed a law banning English words on outdoor signs.

Nearly one-quarter of all Canadians are of French origin. But other languages besides English and French are heard. For example, Gaelic, an ancient tongue of the British Isles, is heard in some Nova Scotia villages. And various East Indian, Middle Eastern, and Oriental dialects are spoken in crowded big cities by the country's newest immigrants.

Education

Two major school systems exist in Canada: the Public School System and the Roman Catholic Separate School Board. Some teach in English and some in French. There are a few French schools in English-speaking Ontario as well as New Brunswick and Manitoba and English schools in Quebec. But Quebec now requires all new immigrant children to attend French schools only.

Public schools offer kindergarten plus 12 grades of education — except in Ontario. There, children take an extra year of high school. This 13-year program is being phased out, but many Ontario teachers and parents believe it better prepares students for work or college.

In all provinces, education is free and compulsory from the ages of five or six through the ages of 17 or 18. Studies consist of language arts, math, science, French, and social studies. Depending on the day of the week, the remaining time is devoted to music, art, or health and physical education and, in the upper grades, home economics or shop.

Requirements for entering the approximately 60 colleges and universities in Canada vary from province to province. A college degree usually takes three to four years to complete.

Population and Ethnic Groups

Canada is one of the few countries that encourages each ethnic or religious group to maintain its identity if it chooses. Since French- and English-speaking populations have kept their separate identities since the founding of the country, this idea has been practically built in to the concept of Canada. So some newcomers keep their lifestyles from foreign countries, while others become what they see as Canadian.

About 40% of all Canadian citizens are of British ancestry. Those of French heritage account for another 24%. The remainder are of other European descents or are a mix of almost every nationality on earth, although many of these eight or nine million Canadians have at least one British ancestor.

About one Canadian of six was born outside Canada. This shows that Canada continues to be a refuge for persons seeking better ways to live. Canadians range from tiny religious sects like the Hutterites to numerous wealthy Chinese who recently arrived because they feared losing money when China takes over Hong Kong in 1997.

About 90% of Canada's estimated 27 million people live within 220 miles (354 km) of the US border. There are about 300,000 Native Canadians on reservations and fewer than 100,000 Inuit. Yet the Inuit, many of whom live in northern Canada, are the fastest-growing minority today because they have the highest birth rate. This growth spurt is due to better health care and more job opportunities as far northern Canada is developed.

Religion

Roman Catholics make up about 47% of all Canadians, with members of various Protestant groups totaling about 40%. About 10% of all Canadians have no religious preference, while the remainder — fewer than 5% — are of various non-Christian religions. Not all Roman Catholics are of French descent. Many Italians in Toronto, for example, are Roman Catholic, and colonies of French Protestants can be found in Quebec and New Brunswick.

Culture

Culturally, Canada has a problem. With its huge neighbor next door, how can it keep from being overrun with Hollywood movies, US network television, and various fads? Canadians today work hard at maintaining their cultural identity and, in fact, export much of their own popular culture to the US.

For example, one highly regarded "US" movie director, Norman Jewison, actually is Canadian. His huge hit *Moonstruck* was filmed in Toronto, even though it portrays life in New York. More and more movies are being filmed in Canadian cities such as Toronto and Vancouver.

The list of famous writers who were born or live in Canada is almost endless. Two who use Canada as the basis of their literature are Margaret Atwood and Robertson Davies. Atwood's poetry and novels deal in part with Canadians' struggles to avoid being overwhelmed by US culture, industries, and environmental problems. Davies' books often describe life in Canadian small towns.

Canada can also be proud of the art forms created by Pacific Coast Native Canadians. Best known by their totem poles, these tribes adorned everything they made with dramatic images of birds, fish, other animals, and more. Completely original, these carved wood or bone items are incredibly valuable and now are usually seen in national museums.

Climate

Canada's weather is as different as the country is large. On the Pacific coast, summers are cool and dry, while winters are mild and wet. The central plains are transformed from snow-covered deserts in the winter to warm cropland in the summer. Snowstorms rage over eastern Canada in winter and fog often covers the land in spring. The Arctic has long, cool summer days and brief winter days as cold as -70°F (-57°C), with the sun a weak dot in the sky.

Land

The second largest country on earth, Canada has a land area of 3,851,790 square miles (9.98 million sq km). The country stretches more than 3,200 miles (5,150 km) from east to west and a similar distance from Ellesmere Island, at the northern tip of Canada, to the United States border.

But dry land isn't all there is to Canada. The country has more fresh water than anywhere else on earth. There are many big rivers, but none more important than the St. Lawrence. It allows ocean-going ships from the Atlantic to travel into the Great Lakes, picking up and dropping off goods on both sides of the border. Other big rivers are the Nelson, Columbia, Peace, Saskatchewan, Churchill, and the Mackenzie, Canada's longest river.

There are rivers of ice, too, called glaciers. They can move huge boulders as they creep forward only a few inches a year. Far to the north, it's impossible to tell where land ends and year-round ice begins. Above the Arctic Circle are large land areas that thaw only a few inches deep in even the warmest summers. About 50% of Canada is permafrost.

Small mountain ranges are found in Quebec, while huge, snowcapped peaks, such as 19,524-foot (5,951-m) Mt. Logan in the Yukon, form the Canadian Rockies. The Rockies separate the dry central plains and the wet west coast.

Canada also has huge amounts of valuable minerals. Many are embedded in a vast area of rock known as the Canadian Shield, a granite plateau covering most of the eastern half of the country. Carved by ancient glaciers, it's covered with rivers, lakes, forests, bogs, and bare rock outcroppings.

Agriculture and Industry

A popular image of Canada is of endless fields of wheat waving in the sun. It's an accurate image — Canada produces much more grain than it can consume, even though only 7% of the land is used to raise crops. Vegetables grow well in southern Ontario, Quebec, and the Maritime Provinces. Almost 12 million cattle, 10 million pigs, a million sheep, and a million tons of fish are raised or caught and processed each year.

Canadians also produce huge quantities of steel, automobiles, machinery, building products, processed food, and paper and wood products. More than one adult in four is in service industries such as fast foods, banking, or communications.

Canada has one of the world's best — and most far-flung — transportation systems. Modern trains carry riders and freight over vast distances. Cities such as Toronto and Montreal have space-age subway systems. Modern airports and superhighways connect major population centers.

Sports

What's the national sport of Canada? If you guessed hockey — you're wrong! While hockey is the country's most popular sport, the official national sport is lacrosse, the ancient Native North American game played on a field by two teams using sticks with cupped nets on one end. As in hockey, each team tries to score goals in the other team's net. Both games are tough, and players wear helmets and padding.

Professional or big-league sports include hockey, baseball, and football. Among children, swimming, cycling, soccer, baseball, and hockey are quite popular. The most popular family sports are boating, fishing, swimming, ice-skating, skiing, and camping.

Hunting and fishing are popular throughout Canada. Polar bears, moose, and other animals are plentiful in remote areas — but so are mosquitoes. In the short, warm arctic and subarctic summers, black flies and mosquitoes can be thicker than almost anywhere on earth!

Currency

Canadian paper money carries portraits of famous Canadians, often prime ministers. The queen of Great Britain is on some bills and on all current coins, including the new $1 coin, which has replaced the $1 bill. The coin is called a "loony" because the side opposite the queen's portrait shows a loon! In 1991, a Canadian dollar was worth 88 cents in US money.

Ottawa

Canada's capital city is at the eastern end of Ontario, the most populous English-speaking province, and next door to Quebec, where nearly everyone speaks French. The city of 320,000 is easy for Ontarian or Québecois to get around in, since signs are, of course, in both official languages.

Towering on a bluff overlooking the Ottawa River, this elegant city features handsome 19th- and 20th-century government buildings, plus galleries, museums, shopping malls, and canals. Parliament Hill, the highest point in Ontario, draws tourists for the Changing of the Guard, a musical ceremony with the guards dressed in scarlet tunics and bearskin hats. Lush parks are scattered throughout the city, many blooming with the four million tulips that the people of Holland sent to Ottawa in thanks for housing the Dutch royal family during World War II. At the city's center stands a 1,200-acre (485-ha) experimental farm with fields, herds of cattle, and an agricultural museum.

While Ottawa's major industries are the government and tourism, it's also a major producer of electronic and communications equipment. Many adults are government employees, living well in a city that is clean and scenic.

Immigrants to Canada

Because it is stable, prosperous, and peaceful, Canada is one of the top three countries in the world in terms of the number of people who immigrate there. The government has been increasing immigration quotas over the past few years. While most immigrants came from Europe in the early 1970s, now many come from Hong Kong, the Philippines, Vietnam, and India.

More Books about Canada

Canada. Bender (Silver Burdett)
Canada. Law (Chelsea House)
Canada. Sirimarco (Rourke)
Canada: Good Neighbor to the World. Bryant (Dillon Press)
We Live in Canada. Brickendon (Franklin Watts)

Glossary of Important Terms

cold war .... the conflict between one group of nations led by the USSR and another group led by the US. Although no actual shots were fired by one group against the other, both groups tried to dominate the politics of other countries since the end of World War II in 1945. With the overthrow in 1989 of communist governments in several eastern European countries long dominated by the USSR, the cold war ended.

Hutterites .... a rural and conservative religious group located primarily in Manitoba and Alberta, Canada.

Inuit .... a group of native people living mainly in several small coastal areas in Greenland, Canada, Alaska, and Siberia.

NATO .... the North Atlantic Treaty Organization; promotes military and economic cooperation among its sixteen European and North American member nations.

parliament .... a body of people with the power to make and change laws; a type of legislature.

permafrost .... permanently frozen layer of earth beneath the surface soil.

precedent .... a model that may be followed later.

Things to Do — Research Projects and Activities

Canada has long been considered a peaceful giant with various ethnic groups working together. But now some of these groups are trying to split off. For example, the French in Quebec are considering separating from the other provinces, and some Native Americans are demanding special rights. For many Canadians, especially those with a strong sense of pride in their ethnic heritage, the question has become: What does it mean to be a Canadian?

As you read more about Canada and its peoples' current struggles to define themselves, be aware of the importance of having current information. Some of the activities and projects below require up-to-date information. Two publications your library may have will tell you about recent magazine and newspaper articles on Canada and other topics:

Readers' Guide to Periodical Literature
Children's Magazine Guide

1. Find where ancient people may have entered Canada from Asia. With a map that shows hills, valleys, rivers, and more, try to understand how difficult it was for them to move across Canada. How many kinds of natural barriers stood in their way? How do modern Canadians over-come such barriers?

2. There are no English-language street signs in Montreal. Which highway signs would be most important if you were a driver there? How do you think having only French signs will affect relations with English-speaking Canadians?

3. With an eye toward the future, how does the next century look for Canada? In what ways is it good or bad? Consider politics, natural resources, the size of the country, and the various ethnic groups.

4. If you would like a Canadian pen pal, write to:

International Pen Friends   Worldwide Pen Friends
P.O. Box 290065   P.O. Box 39097
Brooklyn, NY 11229   Downey, CA 90241

Be sure to tell them from what country you want your pen pal. Also include your name, age, and address.

Index